FONZIE'S BOY

Invisible Hope Series: Book III

Marsha Franks

Illustrations by Elenei Rae Pulido

Print information available on the last page

Rev. date: 03/09/2017

To order additional copies of this book, contact:
Xlibris
1-888-795-4274
www.Xlibris.com
Orders@Xlibris.com

FONZIE'S BOY

Invisible Hope Series: Book III

Marsha Franks

Illustrations by Elenei Rae Pulido

Tyrone James lives on the west side of Birmingham, AL near Ensley. He lives with his mom, Shantel James, and his two sisters, Shaton, 7, and Shala, 9. Tyrone's father left right after he was born. His mom said his dad did not want to have kids anymore so he left them. His father cannot be found to pay child support to his mother. Shaton and Shala's father pays enough child support to keep him out of jail, but he doesn't come around to see them. Shantel works at night for Clean-Pro, cleaning office buildings downtown. She's been with them for two years and the job really helps them get by each month. Shantel is proud she can provide for her family. His sisters stay with the neighbors while his mom is gone at night. He stays at home because he is not afraid to be by himself. Tyrone is five feet four inches tall and is husky built. He refers to himself as the "man of the house" even though he is only ten years old. They don't have much living in the housing projects, but they have what they need.

Tyrone and the girls make good grades in school and stay out of trouble, making their mom proud of them. They want the cell phones and I Pads like the other kids at school, but they understand why their mom cannot get them. Tyrone's grades have fallen some this year, but Shantel believes it is his age and the peer pressure at school to be like everyone else that is causing his grades to slide.

It's Friday night, and Shantel has to go to work.

"Tyrone!" she calls out. "I'm taking the girls next door. What are you doing tonight?"

"I don't know mom, probably just hang around with Ray Charles and Cool Red." Tyrone answered.

"Don't stay out to late" Shantel told him, "and stay out of trouble. See you in the morning."

His mom left with his sisters. He was in the house alone. Tyrone sat on the couch and flipped through the TV channels. He looked at the clock; it was nine pm. He was going to meet Ray Charles at ten o'clock. Tyrone puts his cap on backwards and walks out of the house.

Tyrone digs into the front pockets of his low hung, baggy jeans. "Man! I don't have any more K!" he exclaims. "How am I gonna get money to go to the movie?"

Special K is a drug that makes people hyper and sometimes groggy. Guys will buy it for their girlfriends so they will have more fun. He doesn't care about taking it, but he does take other drugs with his friends. For him it's about making money. He's been selling Special K for months now and can't even remember what he did before this. He has money to hang out with his friends and buy stuff. Shantel is gone at night and sleeps some in the daytime. She has noticed that he is different at times. He smiles as he thinks about how he has fooled his mom. The drug he takes with his friends has been doing a work in his system. Tyrone wants some of the Dust every day now. Tyrone has not noticed he has gotten hooked on cocaine. His mom has told him many times to say no to drugs, but his friends were all into it, making it hard for him to refuse. Shantel wanted him to hang out with "good kids"; those that go to church on Sunday. That is where he met Ray Charles, at a youth meeting. Cool Red is Ray Charles' best friend. They are both 13, and even though he is a few years younger, they took him under their wing. He follows them around and goes places with them. Tyrone has been eager to fit in with them in whatever they do. They are like big brothers to him.

Tyrone turns the corner at the end of the street and Ray Charles is not there yet. They need to go get more Dust for themselves and Special K to sell to the guys they know in the neighborhood that will buy from them. He heard some of the guys they sell to will go sell the K to other people for more money. It profits all of them that way. As long as he makes some money, he doesn't care.

It was ten o'clock, so Tyrone walked on down the street looking for Ray Charles. He saw Ray Charles running towards him. "Hey Ty!" Ray calls to him. "Hey man, we've got to meet Cool Red at a house a few blocks away. Some new guys are there and they are cooking up some new stuff. We are going to try it out for them. A little of it will help us to know how much to sell at one time for a hit. They will pay us to try it."

"I don't think that is a good idea," Tyrone said as he thought about what Ray Charles had said. "We don't know what that stuff would do to us."

"Well, it can't be bad, cause the stuff is selling like crazy at other places! We would only try a little." Ray replied.

"What is the stuff?" Tyrone asked.

"It is called "trash". It gives you a lot of energy and keeps you going for a while as you float around feeling like the world belongs to you." Ray explained. "It is also called meth and people can make it themselves. People will buy it cause it makes them feel good. As long as you take very small amounts, it won't hurt you. You in?

"I guess so." Tyrone said.

As they walked towards the house, Cool Red comes up and joins them.

"Hey man," he says. "I talked with Ritz and they are ready to go with the trash. The house is not too far from here. We will try the stuff, and then get some to sell to others 'cause we can tell them how good it makes us feel."

They walk up to an old abandoned house. There was a strange smell coming from the structure. Ritz met them at the door.

"Hey, good to see 'ya." Ritz said to them as he stuck out his hand to Cool Ray. "Come on in and see what the bank looks like."

The three of them went into the house. Inside the door looks into the kitchen where two men and a woman were cooking something over a portable gas stovetop. At the end of the kitchen area were two small, dirty, blond-haired children playing with some old toys. As Tyrone glanced at the children he though he saw a white figure draped over them. He blinked his eyes and saw two large white angels with their wings spread out around the two children. When he blinked again, the angels were gone.

"Did you see that?" Tyrone asked Ray Charles.

"See what?" Ray Charles asked.

"Forget it." Tyrone said. 'No one will believe what he saw anyway,' he thought.

He focused on the cooking pot. The smell was strong and reminded him of a combination of cigarette smoke and burning alcohol. It almost burned in his throat as he smelled it. On the counter were small rock-like, dirty-white chunks of something.

"This is the trash." Ritz told them. "We are going to try a little bit to see what we will be selling."

Tyrone began to remember his mother's words about saying "no" to drugs. 'He'd just try a tiny bit.' he thought.

Some of the chunks were put in a pipe and passed around. Tyrone barely took a small draw off the pipe. Something inside him told him he didn't need to do this, and he was a little afraid, but he wouldn't let anyone see it.

Ritz took a long draw from the pipe and sat down and waited for the affect. Ray Charles and Cool Red took a draw from it also, but didn't take as much as Ritz.

"Let's go and see what this stuff will do." Ray Charles told Tyrone and Cool Red. They left the house walking back towards the projects. After walking a while, Ray Charles said, "Whew! I'm feeling that! A little dizzy-headed, but I feel like I could fly off that roof top!" he exclaimed.

"I just want to go lie down." Cool Red said.

Tyrone felt a little funny, like he'd just drunk an energy drink and was getting a caffeine high. His mind was wondering and he was seeing creepy things, like bats flying around him. "I don't think I like this trash," he told his friends as he sat down on the sidewalk. "It's different from that other stuff we take."

"Awww, you're just being a baby." Cool Red said. "Just think of the money we can make selling this stuff. Yep, they'll like how this stuff makes 'em feel."

"Yeah," replied Ray Charles, "We could even get phones and I Pads, and other stuff like the rich kids. We're gonna make some dough with this stuff."

"We can meet back with Ritz this weekend for the sales plan." Cool Red said. "See ya tomorrow, I'm goin' home."

"Are you ok Ty boy?" asked Ray Charles.

"All good." Tyrone replied. "Just feeling weird."

"Is it a good weird or bad weird?" Ray Charles asked him.

"It's good." Tyrone said as he started laughing.

"Ok. I'm gonna go home too, see you tomorrow." Ray Charles said. He turned towards the direction of his house.

Tyrone got up and walked down the sidewalk towards his neighborhood. He was still feeling weird; kinda sickly and groggy, but also somewhat giddy and energetic. He rounded a corner and saw a young man leaning up against the building looking towards him. This young man looked like Fonzie from the old Happy Days series on TV. He used to watch the show's reruns with his sisters. He wore jeans that were rolled up past his ankles. The penny-loafer shoes looked new and the white t-shirt was very white. His black hair was slicked back on each side with a lock of hair falling down over his right eye. He looked at Tyrone as he chewed on a stick in his mouth. "Boy," he said. "what are you doin?"

"Goin home," Tyrone answered.

"I mean with that poison you took while ago." the young man said.

"How'd ya know bout that?" Tyrone asked the stranger.

"I just know things." The young man replied.

"Who are you?" Tyrone asked.

"I'm a friend, here to remind you that your life is more important money. That stuff can kill you." the young man said.

"And just who are you and why is this your business?" Tyrone asked trying to sound older than his years.

"My name is Jon. I am here to protect you from hurting yourself?"

"I don't need your protection, man," Tyrone said. "I can take care of myself."

"No, you can't when it comes to this stuff you're taking. This stuff will get you sucked in before you know it and you'll be hooked. You will get where all you care about is taking more of the stuff. You will lose all of yourself to this drug and your life will be wasted. You won't even realize what is happening to you till it is too late. You can die by taking too much at one time. " Jon explained.

"Look Fonzie, or Jon, or whatever your name is, I'll be ok." Tyrone said.

"I tell you what," Jon said, "really look at what is going on around you tomorrow and if you are still ok with it, I'll leave you alone. But, if you are not, I'll be back."

"How do you know what I'm doin' tomorrow?"

"I told you, I just know." Jon replied.

"How will you know what I'm feeling about it?" Tyrone asked.

"I'll know that too." Jon said. "See you later." And Jon walked around the corner of the building and left Tyrone alone to walk the rest of the way home.

Saturday morning, Shantel was asleep in her bed. Shaton and Shala were watching cartoons on TV when Tyrone got up. He got the cereal down from the shelf and fixed some for his sisters and himself. He watched TV with his sisters for a while. His mom was up at lunch time and made sandwiches for them. After lunch, Tyrone told his mom he was goin' to hang out with Ray Charles a while and would be back for supper. He met up with Cool Red and Ray Charles at the edge of the projects.

"That was good stuff!" Cool Red said. "Makes you want to try it again, don't it?"

"It wasn't so bad." Ray Charles replied. "But I got the nervous shakes later on last night that wasn't so good. Maybe, I didn't get a good enough hit when I tried it. How bout you, Ty?"

"It made me feel strange, but good. It took a long time for me to go to sleep." Tyrone said.

They went back to the old house. The same people were there as before. They tried trash again, this time taking a deeper draw from the pipe. Ritz had made a deal for them to sell the drug on the streets. They all got some of the trash to sell. They would get a portion of the money when they brought it back to the house. The drug had a stronger effect on them this time. It will make them bolder out on the streets as they sell it. By supper time, Tyrone had sold all of his supply. He got $100.00 for his work that afternoon. Trash made him feel older and confident out on the street. Although he felt hyper and jumpy, he couldn't tell any negative effects from the drug. Tyrone and his two friends continued for the next two weeks selling the drug and taking it a little of it themselves. Cool Red began taking so much of it because he would have anger fits at times. Ray Charles had to have a few draws from the pipe each day, but tried not to take too much at one time. Tyrone kept taking it till he felt he had to have a draw daily to keep him going. His mom did not know he was taking drugs. He thought he would be alright, and he was making some money.

They went to the house where the drug was being made. In the house the woman and one of the men were working over the gas stove. The second man was sitting up against the wall, his head hung over to one side and his eyes were wide open. He was not moving.

"Is he ok?" Tyrone asked.

"He's fine." the man said. "He's just on a high that has lasted for a while and can't find his way back. He's just having an out-of-this-world-experience."

The two children were there playing at the end of the kitchen as they were every time they came. As Tyrone looked at them, he could see the image of the angels over them. He looked back at the man sitting on the floor. As Tyrone stared at him, Jon walked up from behind him.

"That man has died from taking that stuff." Jon told him. "You need to get out of here and stop smoking this drug."

"Fonzie! Where did you come from," Tyrone asked.

"I could tell, you were wondering what was going on with that guy on thy floor. I sensed a little fear come up inside you. I came to help. No one can see or hear me but you, Tyrone." Jon said.

"What? Why? Who are you?" Tyrone asked him again.

"Let's go outside and I will explain it to you." Jon told him.

"Hey guys," Tyrone said to Ray Charles and Cool Red. "I'm gonna stand outside a few minutes so I can breathe." They looked towards him and nodded as they talked with the man about making money selling this stuff.

Once outside, Jon said. "Tyrone, I am an angel and I am here to protect you from these drugs, because drugs can kill you. That man in there did not think it would kill him, but it did. Tyrone, you are just a kid, there is a lot to life you don't know about yet. Doors can open for you and give you a chance at a better future than you'll ever have here in this neighborhood."

"You don't look like an angel. Those two kids in there have angels watching over them and they have wings and are in white. I saw them. You don't look like them. You look like some punk I saw on an old TV show." Tyrone argued.

"Every child has an angel or two that watches over them. Those two children in there are in danger from their parents cooking that drug. Things can happen that could kill them, but their angels were sent to look over them and protect them till they are delivered from being there." Jon explained. "The police will soon come and take them away from their parents. Those children will be placed in a home where they will be safe."

"How do you know all of this? Why are you here with you me?" Tyrone asked.

"Tyrone, your mother prays for you every night when she goes to work; for your protection, for you to make right choices, and for you to have a great future away from here." Jon said. "Her prayers are why I am here. Angels carry out the prayers that go up to Heaven. Those children are protected because their grandmother prays for them. You saw their angels with them so you would believe what I am telling you. Tyrone, you've got to change your path. Your life is in danger."

"But Ray Charles and Cool Red are my friends; I don't have anyone else." Tyrone said as he hung his head.

"Doors will open if you go in the right direction, Tyrone." Jon said to him. "Get involved more with the youth at church and get to know the youth minister. You can show them how strong you really are by walking away from all of this. If Ray Charles and Cool Red are really your friends, let them follow you."

"What if they don't?" Tyrone asked.

"Your choices decide your future, Tyrone. They make their own choices. But you have to live your life and let them live theirs. If their choices are bad and they continue taking drugs, their fate could mean a short life." Jon replied. "I'm here to tell you, you can have a better life than you can imagine. You don't have to stay in this neighborhood forever."

"Ok, I understand. But, leaving my friends won't be easy." Tyrone replied.

"I know." Jon said rubbing his head with his fist. "But you are stronger than you think, and you will be okay." They began to walk down the sidewalk away from the house. Tyrone was silent for a while as they walked.

Looking down, Tyrone asked laughing, "Where did you get those shoes, anyway?"

Jon just looked at him and laughed.

The next Sunday, Tyrone was at the youth group. He decided to follow Jon's advice. After all, he thought, who would be more street-wise than Fonzie? He thought about that old TV show where the neighborhood boys looked up to Fonzie. Fonzie would give the boys good advice. Thinking about the show, Tyrone suddenly leaned back and shouted, "Heyyyy!" and put his hands out like Fonzie would do on the show. He laughed at himself.

Printed in the United States
By Bookmasters